I0555321

Issue 5
MUSINGS

Fashion

WEDNESDAYCORE
Ghost City x Killstitch
Lettoria Handbags

Art

An Unmapped Experience in
Graffiti Art by our NYC It Girl

Music

Rock n' Soul Tarot by NY
Shark Radio Host Brian
Orlando

Entertainment

15 Spooky Influencers to
Follow Including:
@rebysky
@beforethecoffin
@witchvoid
@blairscares
@christinaakaiser
and more!
An exclusive look at
Parahouse Magazine

EDITOR'S NOTE

I've been doing internal PR work with a great group of 'ghost guys' lately, so I wanted this issue to honor an interest of mine: the unknown. Welcome to FAME's exclusive Halloween issue, because Wednesday Addams is trending, afterall. I hope you enjoy the intersect where goth meets glamour, and knowledge is chic.

While I have spent nearly 15 years working in the realms of fashion, art, music, and entertainment - there was a part of me that I left behind. I grew up with a love for history, mysteries, and the otherworldy. So much of my childhood was spent with my grandfather strolling cemeteries, deep diving into the heritage of our early Scottish settlers, or talking about the very real possibility of time travel. Nonetheless, knowledge and a love for the world's adventures was always instilled in me.

Charissa Lauren

Editor-in-Chief

In this issue

Charissa Lauren, Editor-in-Chief
Kathy Copcutt, Travel & Beauty Editor
Jeanine Pederson, NYC IT Girl
Jennifer Adams Keith, LA IT Girl
Photography Contributors: Justin Hreha, Cover: Dan Santoni, Life Passion Photography

PATTI
NEGRI

Maybe you've seen her a time or two. Best known for her recurring role on Ghost Adventures, she is also the author of Old World Magick for the Modern World and now, Dollcraft, in which she explores the lore, practical magic, protection rituals for haunted dolls, and even recipes and poppet magick.

Her ability to weave together heartfelt storytelling, metaphysical insight, and practical guidance has earned her acclaim as a leading psychic-medium and "Good Witch." Her work has appeared on television, radio, and through her many books and podcasts.

CELEBRITY SPOTLIGHT

Q: Patti, thanks for gracing the cover of FAME Magazine this season. You're known as the "Good Witch of Hollywood." Tell us about your gift and when you started to notice your unique talents.

A: *I've always known. Even as a little girl, I was talking to spirits and energies, and I honestly think most kids can—except it gets taught out of us in our modern, left-brain, non-mystical society. But it wasn't taught out of me. My mom encouraged it; she'd say, "Yes, your grandma could see that too," or "Grandma could do that as well." It was embraced, welcomed, and allowed to grow.

I was always fascinated by the other side—not in a dark or morbid way, but with pure curiosity. I literally did my first séance when I was seven or eight years old because I knew spirits had a lot to say, and I wanted to give them that chance. Some kids are born knowing how to sing—I was born knowing how to connect with the other side. And that's really where it all began...*

Q: How did you begin to develop your abilities and build a career as a psychic medium?

A: *I've always been a seeker. I wasn't raised with any religion or spirituality—in fact, my grandfather was a well-known psychoanalyst and philosopher, a very staunch atheist humanist. But as a child, whenever we passed a church, mosque, or temple, I could feel the energy radiating from it. I longed to go inside and experience it.

15 minutes with FAME

You can follow patti at @patti.negri on Instagram
Photos by Life Passion Photography

At thirteen, I asked my mom if I could explore a house of worship, and she said yes. That freedom started my lifelong spiritual journey. In the 1980s, I attended a women's spirit circle in Long Beach and discovered the Wiccan path. Their deep connection to nature felt like home to me.

Over time, I grew beyond labels—today, I wouldn't call myself strictly Wiccan because my practice embraces many magical traditions. But at the core, my work is elemental, rooted in earth, air, fire, and water. I've studied with incredible teachers all over the world, and I'm still learning every day. The more you know, the more you realize how much magic there is left to discover.*

Q: You've appeared for several years on one of America's favorite paranormal shows, Ghost Adventures. What has been the best part about working with the team?

A: *It's all been amazing. I love adventure, and I love a challenge—and working with Zak Bagans and the team is always both! I never know where I'm going. At best, I get an address or a plane ticket, but I don't know the history of the place, which means I go in fresh, with no expectations clouding my intuition.

That's the thrill: walking into some of the most haunted, magical locations on Earth and experiencing them raw. The team itself is wonderful—such professionals and such a family. I feel like the luckiest girl in the world to have been working with them for over a decade now, usually two episodes a year. It's always a highlight of my life.*

Q: You recently released the book Dollcraft: A Witch's Guide to Poppet Magick and Haunted Dolls. How did you get into haunted dolls?

A: *I've loved dolls my entire life. I've been a collector since birth—probably even in utero! If you look around my office, there are hundreds of little eyes looking back at me. Most are Barbie dolls, and interestingly, I've never had a haunted Barbie. I think she's such a goddess in her own right that she doesn't need to house any other spirits.

My haunted doll work really came into public view when Zak Bagans invited me to do a séance with Peggy the Doll, who was notorious for making people ill—over eighty documented cases, even from just looking at her picture online. That opened the door.

Soon after, a woman in Belgium sent me Belle, my most famous haunted doll, because Belle had been making her sick for years. She asked if I wanted her, and of course I said yes. Once I cleared the dark spirit, Belle became a beloved part of my family.

With Hollywood's fascination with haunted dolls—Annabelle, Robert the Doll, Peggy—I saw a need for a real guidebook. Dollcraft is both a how-to manual for caring for haunted dolls and a book on poppet magick, bridging my paranormal work with my witchy spellcraft. It was a natural fit.*

Q: Speaking of haunted dolls, what is your take on Annabelle? Do you believe she's as evil as all proclaim?

A: *Yes, I do believe Annabelle has a very dark side. Not long ago, I was at a Warrens event, and my booth was set up directly in front of Annabelle and the rest of their haunted collection, separated only by a curtain. The energy was so strong, I had to layer on serious warding just to get through the weekend. It worked—by the end of the day, I was literally dancing in front of Annabelle's glass case!

©Dan Sentoni

That said, I think her energy can be controlled. She is powerful, but she's also in good hands. My dear friends Elton Castee and Matt Rife recently purchased the Warrens' estate, including Annabelle. Not everyone realizes it, but they are both well-trained paranormal investigators. In fact, Elton wrote the very first endorsement for my Dollcraft book. Knowing Annabelle is under their care gives me peace.*

Q: What has been one of the most memorable experiences or haunted locations since you've been in this industry?

A: *There are so many, but the spookiest is definitely the Cecil Hotel in Los Angeles. I've filmed there more than anyone—two Ghost Adventures episodes, a four-episode overnight with Elton's team, even a CW show. The energy is just… heavy. Out of 700 rooms, each one carries its own layer of sadness, depression, or hopelessness.

I would love to see it cleared, but it would probably take every healer, priest, rabbi, witch, and medicine person on the planet to surround it and flood it with love and light.

I also love traveling east to explore America's haunted history, and even further to Europe, where the spirits are older and the castles go back centuries. From Los Angeles to London, there's adventure everywhere in the spirit world.*

Q: What would you advise to anyone upcoming who may have similar gifts but they're unsure of where to go next?

A: *First—check out my online school, University Magickus. We started it about five years ago, and it's truly the most affordable spiritual and magical school out there. Classes are as little as $10–$20 and taught live on Zoom. I teach psychic development, mediumship, spellcasting—you name it. And we have brilliant teachers worldwide, sharing everything from Strega magic in Italy to Philippine witchcraft, Reiki, astrology, tarot, and more.

The only rule: no one can say, "This is the truth." They can only say, "This is my truth." That way, students are exposed to many paths and can find what resonates.
Beyond my school, I'd say: follow your heart. Go to bookstores, take classes, seek out teachers. We live in a time where the mystical arts are more accessible than ever. Take advantage of it.*

Q: Tell us about the sessions you offer.

A: *I offer private sessions, which can be 30 or 60 minutes, and I also have coaching packages for those who want ongoing guidance. Sessions can focus on psychic development, mediumship, spiritual clearings—whatever a client needs, since it's based on time.

> "

PATTI NEGRI

MY DEAR FRIENDS ELTON CASTEE AND MATT RIFE RECENTLY PURCHASED THE WARRENS' ESTATE, INCLUDING ANNABELLE. NOT EVERYONE REALIZES IT, BUT THEY ARE BOTH WELL-TRAINED PARANORMAL INVESTIGATORS. IN FACT, ELTON WROTE THE VERY FIRST ENDORSEMENT FOR MY DOLLCRAFT BOOK. KNOWING ANNABELLE IS UNDER THEIR CARE GIVES ME PEACE.

"

Gina BLACK

Gina & her new book: Etched in Stone – Decoding Hidden Meanings in Cemeteries

Gina Black is a paranormal investigator and author from South Florida. She enjoys investigating haunted locations and iconic historic cemeteries as the co-founder of Afterlife Allstars and Author of Etched in Stone. Some favorites include Pennhurst State School, the Lizzie Borden House, Stanley Hotel, and White Hill Mansion.
Check out her adventures on Instagram at @SheHaunts and SheHaunts.com

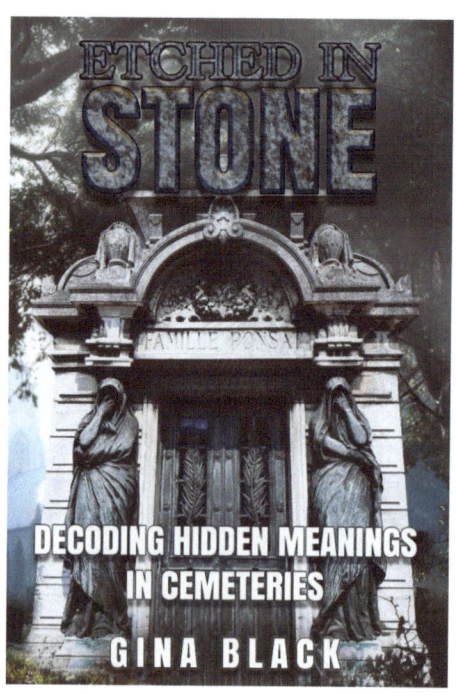

Spooky Influencers to follow

On entering the tourism industry primarily focusing on haunted history, I was acquainted with so many talented women who carry such a passion for this work. It is inspiring to work within a group of women who have a yearn for knowledge, history, and the peculiar. There is something to be said about those who stay curious in life - it is a magic I wish everyone had. -CL

Reby Sky Hardy
@rebysky

Reby Hardy is an author, game designer, former pro wrestler, model & pianist/composer, writing & performing several original scores for various television programs, including WWE Raw & AEW Dynamite.

Her popular web series "Life of a Gothic Baby" has transformed into a best selling childrens book of the same title.

Reby is a full time spooky content creator whose passion stems from a lifelong desire to tell creative & entertaining stories. Her dry, comedic timing & vast experience across all nearly forms of entertainment & media makes for original content that stands out in a sea of modern day influencers.

DIXIE HARTZOG
@WITCHVOID

Dixie is an enthusiastic travel influencer with a passion for exploring "off the beaten path." Her content highlights haunted hotspots, rich history, and hidden gems around the world. With a degree in Filmmaking and a love for the macabre, Dixie crafts immersive, thrilling stories through the art of content creation—giving followers a unique travel experience and inspiring them to visit extraordinary places.

HEATHER TAYLOR
@BEFORETHECOFFIN

Heather Taylor - an alternative travel creator with a background in death care spanning eight years, and a lifelong devotee of horror cinema. Her work blends a fascination with the macabre and the unique, spotlighting unusual destinations, historic sites, and cultural traditions often overlooked by mainstream travel.

BLAIR SCARES
@BLAIRSCARES

Blair Scares—known as "your favorite dream and your worst nightmare"—is the host of The Blair Scares Horror Show, a platform celebrating everything from cult classics to cutting-edge indie gems. Blair shines a spotlight on horror's most passionate creators, bringing the genre's thrills to life in a fun and engaging way. With a special love for indie horror, Blair has partnered with film festivals across the U.S., mingling with filmmakers, championing their visions, and connecting their work with eager new audiences hungry for the next scare.

CHRISTINA KAISER
@CHRISTINAAKAISER

Christina—also known as Chrissy—creates content that blends her love of vintage fashion, nostalgic media, and the paranormal. Her passion began in childhood, from watching classic shows like Three's Company and admiring 1970s style, to her first viewing of The Conjuring in 2013, which deepened her fascination with the unexplained. She expresses herself through whimsical media, from fantasy films to dressing as beloved book characters, and never misses a chance to browse antique stores for records or vintage dresses. Since starting to share her favorite things in 2020, Chrissy has built a community where fans of these unique niches can connect, feel seen, and celebrate their shared interests. She's excited to see where the journey takes her next.

VIVA
@VIVA_LA_MELISA

Brooklyn-born and raised, Viva has spent over a decade investigating some of the most haunted locations in the United States. Her fascination with the paranormal began early, inspired by her mother's own passion for the unexplained. While she describes herself as a smaller voice in the influencer world, her drive, curiosity, and dedication to uncovering the unknown push her far beyond the ordinary—and toward a future even she can't yet envision.

HALEY MICHELLE
@MISSHALEYMICHELLE

Also known as the Paranormal Princess, is an Indiana native who discovered her profound connection to the paranormal at a young age. As she explored this fascination, she uncovered her innate psychic abilities, enabling her to facilitate healing connections between individuals and their deceased loved ones. Furthermore, she compassionately communicates with the trapped souls within her collection of haunted dolls. Through Tiktok, she shares her inspiring experiences, connections, and passion for the paranormal with her rapidly growing community of 2.9 million followers.

ORLANDO

BRIAN ORLANDO

ROCK 'n SOUL TAROT

Interpreting the Cards
Through the Universal
Language of Music

Self-Discovery

Intuition

Foreword by
Skid Row's David "Snake" Sabo

Afterword by
Candlebox's Kevin Martin

You can order Rock n'
Soul Tarot on Amazon &
Barnes & Noble

Rock n' Soul Tarot

By Brian Orlando

Brian, tell us about when you first entered the music scene. How did you end up in radio?

I fell in love with music before I ever learned to walk. My father was dancing with me to Heart Of Glass by Blonide in order to get me to fall asleep. My Uncle who was a teenager at the time would impress his college friends by having me sing the entire Meet the Beatles album in between swigs of Apple Juice from my sippy cup. When I was six, My stepmother put on Iron Man by Black Sabbath and my world changed forever. I always wanted to be IN music but couldn't play an instrument or sing to save my life. Believe me I tried. I had always relied on the radio DJ's to get me through my truck driving routes. One day when I was 28, I entered a contest for free tuition for a local broadcasting school. I didn't win, but at that point I was committed, so I took out an awful deal on a loan, enrolled in the school and never looked back. While in school, one of my instructors, Rich Desisto invited me to do weekends on the rock radio station he programmed. It was truly my "big break."

You have a pretty impressive career. Of all the artists you've interviewed, what is one interview that sticks out?

Well now there's a lot of noise in my head because about 30 started playing back in my head at the same time and all for different reasons. Since I was 15, Candlebox has been a major influence on me. From friends their music helped me make to memories that were made while their CD was playing, they were just a constant in my life.

Throughout the years I had the chance to interview the lead singer, Kevin Martin many times over the years but back in 2015, he thanked ME at the end of an interview for always supporting his band. This is a guy who got me through the roughest times of my life and here he is telling me about what I did for HIM. I never forgot that.

As far as prestige, there is no bigger rock band in my eyes than ACDC. I walked into the studio on the day of the interview on zero sleep. I was too excited and I was in disbelief that this was really happening. Even after hundreds of interviews. The phone rang and I went BLANK. Brian must have heard my voice crack so he started with "I gotta tell you Brian, you might be the first DJ I ever met and I've been around quite a bit. I think that's pretty cool" You couldn't pry the smile off of my face for weeks.

BRIAN ORLANDO

MUSIC IS A CONNECTOR. YOU CAN WIND UP TALKING TO A TOTAL STRANGER FOR HOURS IN A SUPERMARKET AISLE IF THEY HAPPEN TO BE WEARING YOUR FAVORITE BANDS T-SHIRT. MUSIC REPRESENTS EMOTIONS AND EXPERIENCES. TAROT DOES THE SAME THING. EACH CARD REPRESENTS SOMETHING WE ALL HAVE GONE THROUGH.

You share a lot in your first book, "Rock n' Soul Tarot," what was the writing process like for you and why did you decide to write the book?

It was all done within about three full weeks. I wrote in coffee shops and kava bars after work. Much of it was written in a BBQ spot called Dang while wolfing down their renown "trash can chips." Some chapters were written at 2 am before work. I knew the format would be covering the 22 cards of the major arcana with songs, and stories. I realized quickly another 56 stories from my life and career would have been agonizing so I stuck with just the songs to help the reader figure out the meanings. I honestly never saw the chapters in my head about the different situations a psychic might encounter until I wrote each one. I'd wake up at 1 am hearing "Should I allow readings to be taped" and just start typing. The stories from my career that I chose were coming out in real time. Some of this stuff I hadn't thought about in years. I was cathartic and it helped me realize just how much of a career I had so far

Markos D1

Markos D1, a.k.a. "The One," is an LA-based pop artist, model, and beauty entrepreneur with a global following. Since 2013, he's collaborated with legendary producers like Grammy-nominated DJ Kane (Kumbia Kings) and Grammy-winner Chris Pérez to create hits like "Borracho," the viral "vuela vuela 2.0," and his latest single, "Ya No." Markos D1 is also a professional model and celebrity socialite who can take your brands to the next level with his social status. Next up, he's set to release two albums—one in English and one in Spanish—and he's gearing up for an epic tour. Follow him on social @MarkosD1official to keep up with the latest

His new single 'Single Again' released in August 2025 and is available on all major streaming platforms.

MUSIC

New Single!

NYC IT GIRL IN PHILLY: AN UNMAPPED EXPERIENCE IN GRAFFITI ART

By Jeanine Pedersen

Many of us have bucket list items that we keep on reserve while traveling. I finally got to visit one of mine! As an avid graffiti and street art enthusiast, Graffiti Pier in Philadelphia is an incredibly unique area located on the Delaware River. The timing never seemed to work out; from bad weather, to traffic, and location, something would always delay my visit.

The best part is you enter at a non-descript point, it's almost secretive! There are no signs directing you and it really is a hidden gem. So, I wanted to go with others from a safety point of the unknown. Imagine my excitement when the stars aligned, I had friends to join me, it was a beautiful day, and we had time.

The background? It is a former coal loading dock transformed into a colorful and vibrant outdoor and public universe of graffiti art. An optical illusion forms as you gaze through the pillars, and the area appears to go on for infinity. You can spend countless inspiring hours deciphering the tags, characters, meanings, and artists. Graffiti also changes, so the space is evolving each time you visit.

Slabs of concrete become the canvas, and artists and urban explorers continue to visit. In 2024 part of the pier collapsed and the land is currently up for sale, now surrounded by new real estate.

While its fate is yet to be determined, I am hopeful that the commissions will preserve this vicinity as a park. Interestingly enough, graffiti is now beginning on the rocks in an adjacent area.

Unfortunately, in the example of 5 Pointz in New York City that was not the case, and it was whitewashed/covered and demolished without notice. Remember you can see the next generation of 5Pointz at the Citizen M NYC on the Bowery at the Museum of Street Art (MOSA) in the stairways. #savetheart

Follow @dressedtothej9s on Instagram to follow NYC's IT Girl for all things style, sports, events, and street art!

Written by Jeanine Pedersen

LEVIATHAN'S LOFT

Leviathan's Loft is where horror meets hygiene.
Specializing in handcrafted soaps, chapsticks and
other bath and body creations, each product is made
from only the best skin-loving ingredients and
infused with a bit of macabre. Ghoul owned and
operated, check out leviathansloft.company.site to
see where you can find them lurking this spooky
season.
Because even monsters need a little me-time.

Meet Justin Hreha: The Lens Elevating Pittsburgh's Fashion Scene

In a city better known for steel than style, Justin is helping put Pittsburgh on the fashion map - blending editorial edge with a distinctly local backdrop. His recent projects include the Ecolution Show, La Fleur at Phipps, and Pittsburgh Fashion Week, showcasing his ability to craft images that feel as at home in Vogue as they do on Pittsburgh's streets.

Book at www.hrehaphotography.com

Created by
Melisa S. Kennedy

PARAHOUSE MAGAZINE: WHERE THE STRANGE AND SPOOKY THRIVE

In a world overflowing with predictable content, *ParaHouse Magazine* stands out as a beacon for those who crave the eerie, the mysterious, and the delightfully unsettling. This bold publication, available both in print and online, has carved a unique niche in the realm of speculative fiction, horror, and the paranormal. With its captivating blend of high-quality storytelling, striking visuals, and a fearless dive into the unknown, *ParaHouse Magazine* is a must-read for anyone who finds beauty in the bizarre. At the heart of its digital presence lies the *Midnight Archive*, a chilling collection of creepypasta stories that will keep you up long past the witching hour.

ParaHouse is also thrilled to announce our newest electrifying collaboration with Haunted Happy Hour Inc., the dynamic duo of sisters Lili and Vanessa, who have infused the world of paranormal podcasts and spirited brews with their signature blend of history, hauntings, and high- quality coffee. This partnership birthed the limited-edition *ParaHouse Ritual Roast*, a truly haunted coffee bundle that spent 13 days and 13 nights absorbing the ethereal "spirits" of Salem's legendary House of the Seven Gables— marking the 333rd anniversary of the Salem Witch Trials with a pour that's as mysterious as it is invigorating.

Packaged in an exclusive one-of-a-kind wooden collector's coffin box, this small-batch roasted delight offers unique, spirited flavors perfect for fans who crave Halloween vibes year-round, blending *ParaHouse's* expertise in the paranormal, witchy, and unexplained with Haunted Happy Hour's innovative coffee craftsmanship. As female-owned brands leading their industries, we're beyond excited to deliver this first-of-its-kind magazine collaboration, where every sip summons a ritual of flavor and fright—preorders kicked off on Friday the 13th of June, inviting you to elevate your morning brew into a supernatural experience. You may order our limited- edition coffee exclusively online at www.hauntedhappyhourqc.com.

As you can already see, *ParaHouse Magazine* is more than just a publication—it's an experience. Each issue is a carefully curated journey into the strange, blending fiction, eyewitness reports, and many kinds of explorations in the paranormal.

Whether you're a lifelong fan of horror or simply curious about the unexplained, *ParaHouse* offers something for everyone. From short stories that twist your perception of reality to in-depth articles exploring urban legends, cryptids, and haunted histories, the magazine delivers a spine-tingling mix of content that's as thought-provoking as it is entertaining.

What sets *ParaHouse* apart is its commitment to quality and creativity. The magazine showcases both established authors and emerging voices, ensuring a

"A Magazine Like No Other! We invite you to join the ParaHouse experience, if you dare." - Melisa

---

diverse range of perspectives and styles. Its pages are adorned with haunting illustrations and photography that amplify the eerie atmosphere of the stories. Whether you're flipping through a physical copy or scrolling through the sleek digital edition, *ParaHouse* immerses you in a world where the line between reality and nightmare blurs. We are accessible to readers worldwide. Subscriptions offer exclusive content, behind-the-scenes looks at the creative process, and early access to new releases.

Unlike the sprawling, unfiltered corners of the internet where creepypastas often originate, the *Midnight Archive* is a carefully crafted space. Each story is selected for its ability to evoke dread, spark curiosity, or leave readers questioning what's lurking just out of sight. From ghostly apparitions in abandoned towns to sinister entities hiding in plain sight, the stories in the *Midnight Archive* are as varied as they are terrifying.

Let us lure you into a shadowy realm of bone-chilling creepypastas, eerie magazines, and spectral coffee.

What makes the *Midnight Archive* truly special is its accessibility. Available for just $5 per month on the *ParaHouse Magazine* website, these stories are perfect for a quick scare during a lunch break or a late-night binge when the house is too quiet. The archive is adding new haunts every Monday with fresh tales, ensuring there's always a new nightmare waiting to be discovered. Readers can also submit their own creepypastas, giving aspiring writers a chance to share their darkest creations with a global audience.

For those who prefer the tactile thrill of a printed magazine, physical copies are available for order, making *ParaHouse* the perfect addition to any coffee table or late-night reading session.

The Midnight Archive: Creepypasta That Haunts

At the core of *ParaHouse Magazine*'s online presence is the *Midnight Archive*, a digital treasure trove of creepypasta stories designed to unsettle and captivate. Creepypastas—short, user-generated horror stories born on the internet—have become a cultural phenomenon, and ParaHouse has elevated the genre to new heights. The *Midnight Archive* is a curated collection of original tales that push the boundaries of fear, imagination, and storytelling.

In an era where content is often churned out for clicks, *ParaHouse Magazine* and its online *Midnight Archive* stand as a testament to the power of storytelling. The magazine doesn't just aim to scare—it seeks to inspire, provoke, and connect. Its stories tap into universal fears and curiosities, reminding us that the unknown is a part of the human experience. Whether it's a tale of a

delivered straight to your inbox or doorstep. Visit the *Midnight Archive* on our website, ever-growing collection of creepypastas that will make you think twice about turning off the light.

Or if you're daring enough, drink in the spirit of *ParaHouse* with our coffee - filled with the haunted history of Salem!

ParaHouse weaves a spellbinding tapestry of horror, mystery, and the paranormal, captivating thrill-seekers with chilling creepypastas, haunting visuals, and the exclusive ritual roast coffee.

---

haunted mirror or an article dissecting the psychology of fear, *ParaHouse* invites readers to embrace the strange and find wonder in the shadows.

If you're ready to dive into a world of the strange and supernatural, *ParaHouse Magazine* and the *Midnight Archive* are waiting for you. Subscribe to the magazine for a regular dose of high-quality horror and paranormal content,

ParaHouse Magazine is more than a publication—it's a community for those who find joy in the eerie and unexplained. Whether you're a casual reader or a die-hard horror aficionado, there's a place for you in the ParaHouse Universe. Visit www.ParaHouseMagazine.com today to start your journey into the unknown. *ParaHouse Magazine,* haunted coffee and the *Midnight Archive* are calling—dare to answer?

Killstitch x Ghost City

Where eerie meets edgy. Killstitch Apparel is the official clothing line from Ghost City, blending darkly inspired gothic glamour with modern streetwear silhouettes. Each piece is crafted for those who love the thrill of the unexplained — think bold graphics, premium fabrics, and subtle nods to the supernatural.

PITTSBURGH FASHION WEEK

Pittsburgh marked 15 years of fashion this year with a couture street-style shoot in the heart of Market Square, a moment that instantly transported me back to 2010, when I was coordinating shows alongside the original founder, Miyoshi Anderson. Few people know this, but that event was truly my first step into PR and media. I was just 20 years old, probably with no business running opening night for one of the city's largest events, yet I was entrusted with the task.

Since then, Pittsburgh Fashion Week has grown tremendously. Under the stewardship of Ronda Zegarelli, Diamonds by Rothschild, and the Pittsburgh Downtown Partnership, it continues to evolve while keeping its loyal community at heart.

This year looked a little different, but our city's fashion lovers still showed up for the designers, proving the strength of an industry in a city better known for sports and steel.

Over the years, I've witnessed designers hone their craft and new talent emerge, all while friendships and connections have formed around a shared love of style. That bond, our "tiny but mighty" fashion family, is the glue that holds Fashion Week together.

So while 2024 didn't bring a runway show, it did bring a moment to reflect on how far Pittsburgh's fashion scene has come — stitched together by creativity, passion, and the fans who make it thrive.

Lettoria